T0274808

AQUAFABA

ACKNOWLEDGEMENTS

This book is dedicated to all pioneers who push the boundaries to keep our world going forward. Thank you to Joël Roessel for being one of these people. All honour and glory to him! Many thanks to Laetitia and Tristan for their constant support and precious friendship. We would also like to thank Wismer (www.wismer.fr) for the use of their equipment.

This English language edition published in 2018 by
Grub Street
4 Rainham Close
London
SW11 6SS

Email: food@grubstreet.co.uk
Twitter: @grub_street
Facebook: Grub Street Publishing
Web: www.grubstreet.co.uk

A CIP record for this title is available from the British Library

ISBN 978-1-911621-15-7

Printed and bound by Finidr, Czech Republic

AQUAFABA

Vegan cooking without eggs using the magic
of chickpea water

SÉBASTIEN **KARDINAL** and LAURA **VEGANPOWER**
Photography by LAURA **VEGANPOWER**

GRUB STREET • LONDON

CONTENTS

WHAT IS
AQUAFABA?

From the Latin *aqua* (water) and *faba* (bean), aquafaba is basically the leftover liquid from cooked legumes. It's incredible to think that this precious liquid that we usually tip down the drain actually has some amazing properties.

Of course, this leftover liquid is primarily composed of water, but it also contains protein, fibre, starch and sugar. During the cooking process around 5% of the natural nutrients in the legumes are transferred to the water. By evaporating the water we can get a higher concentration of these nutrients, thereby reaching an average ratio of 90% water to 10% protein and starch.
This is the exact same ratio that we find in chicken egg whites.
The similarities in the composition of these two liquids explains, in part, why aquafaba reacts in the same way when whisked.
The abundance of tensioactive proteins means that when it is whisked, a superb mousse is obtained that holds its own against the peaks of traditional egg whites.

Technically, aquafaba can be obtained from the cooking juices of most legumes: broad beans, white beans, kidney beans, flageolet, adzuki beans, yellow soy beans, lupin beans, any type of lentil, split peas and, of course, chickpeas.
But, chickpeas are the most commonly used for various reasons. Firstly, raw chickpea aquafaba isn't poisonous, unlike other kinds, and can therefore be used in both its raw and cooked forms. Secondly, it is neutral both in taste and in colour: an essential quality that means it can be used in sweet or savoury recipes. Lastly, it is cheap, easy to make at home and keeps well. For all of these reasons, in this book we have chosen only to use chickpea aquafaba.

For all that, aquafaba isn't a miracle product that substitutes all the qualities of egg whites. We have carried out many tests and experiments to gain a better understanding of aquafaba's behaviour

and how we can use it. While it is true that it can work wonders, there have also been some disappointments. A simple experiment illustrates this well: heat a frying pan to 60 °C with some oil or fat and pour 30 ml of aquafaba at room temperature into the pan.

What happens? It quickly boils and evaporates leaving a fine coated surface on the bottom of the pan. With egg whites, we would have got thick, coagulated whites, supple and pearly. We can't replace ovalbumin completely! When heated, aquafaba disappears quickly if it isn't used with another ingredient like sugar, guar gum, cream of tartar, agar-agar or even a starch... This structural fragility presented us with many challenges and a few real failures.

Take our attempt to make a vegan cheese soufflé for example. It's one of the few savoury recipes that uses whisked egg whites. So it seemed both logical and exciting to give it a go. But nothing could be done! Once in the oven, the soft white peaks of the aquafaba liquefied and dissolved the entire mix. Even with the help of starch or gum, it still didn't work. The same went for the blinis and duchess potatoes. Basically, whisked aquafaba without sugar doesn't like to be cooked! Who knows, maybe in the future some genius in the kitchen will come up with a solution to the problem.

HOW WAS IT
DISCOVERED?

A true culinary revolution dawned in the small world of vegan cuisine: someone discovered a way to create the soft peaks of whisked egg whites... without eggs! From that moment on there was a before and after aquafaba. A border had come crashing down and we suddenly had access to a new, previously forbidden, promised land. The scope of new possibilities was truly staggering! We had come so close without ever realising it... We even thought it could be a hoax: it all just seemed too straightforward. However, the proof was there, right before our eyes, this fabulous ingredient that would change everything...

It all began in late 2014, in France, thanks to Joël Roessel who made the amazing discovery. However, he wasn't a chemist, or a professional chef, or even a specialist in molecular cuisine. Joël is a singer, a tenor, with curiosity and determination in equal measure.
This vegan blogger decided to start testing everything he could get his hands on to obtain a vegan mousse that was dense and stable enough to make one of his favourite dishes: îles flottantes. But, what could he use instead of the whisked egg whites? This is a key challenge that many vegan food lovers have gone to great lengths to overcome using flaxseed decoctions, pure soya protein, CO_2 cartridges and other imaginative ideas. Unfortunately, up until that moment, nobody had managed to find a vegan alternative to the soft peaks of whisked egg whites, that held firm in both its raw and cooked forms. By experimenting with different liquids to try and get a mousse, Joël Roessel found that the viscous liquid drained from a tin of chickpeas, reacted just like egg whites...

He shared this discovery on his blog 'Révolution végétale' (Green revolution), but unfortunately the news took a few months to reach the general public's ears. In fact, it was a video recipe for chocolate mousse, posted by an association that put the spotlight on Joël's technique. From that moment onwards, the news spread like wildfire on social networks. Culinary bloggers threw themselves into a series of tests, putting the theory into practice. At VG-Zone.net, we also got caught up in this wave of creativity making a series of meringues, chocolate mousse, îles flottantes, meringue pie, etc. We became ever more amazed at the simplicity and effectiveness of the technique.

Next, the idea spread through the United States with Goose Wohlt, the man who is credited with the popularisation of the term 'aquafaba', continuing Joël's work. It's a bit more practical and sexier a name than 'the leftover liquid from cooking legumes'!
The English-speaking social networks took care of the rest...
Nowadays, aquafaba has become an ingredient in its own right in the world of vegan cuisine and we wonder how we survived for so long in the dark, deprived of the sweet comfort of its soft peaks.

If you want to experiment by replacing egg whites in recipes from other cookbooks the rough equivalent is 3 tablespoons of aquafaba equals approx. one whole egg, while 2 tablespoons of aquafaba equals approx. one egg white.

WHERE CAN I FIND
AQUAFABA?

———

At the moment of writing, as yet, no brand has commercialised ready-to-use aquafaba. But, we have no doubt that, in the future, we'll be able to buy aquafaba directly, perhaps in cartons or as dehydrated flakes. We're just not quite there yet...

Fortunately, aquafaba is very easy to get your hands on, so long as you like eating chickpeas! There are three ways to obtain it.

The most common way: tinned chickpeas.
As you can buy them anywhere, from your local grocer's right up to huge hypermarkets, buying in tins is the easiest way to get hold of aqua-faba quickly. The advantage of tinned chickpeas is that there are usually only three ingredients: chickpeas, water and salt. Although it's quite rare, keep an eye out for brands that add dubious flavours and additives! The strained liquid is fairly thin and a large 800 g tin usually yields around 250 ml aquafaba.

The qualitative way: chickpeas in a jar.
They are a bit harder to find, but this alternative to tinned chickpeas is meant to be healthier and tastier. To find them, you may have to resort to organic shops or specialist shops. The liquid from a jar of chickpeas is thicker, but there is a lot less of it. If you're not so fussed about trying the delicious chickpeas, it isn't the most economical way.

Home-made: dried chickpeas, to be cooked at home.
It can't be stressed enough: nothing beats home-made cuisine. The same goes for chickpeas. By cooking them yourself, you'll be able to obtain around 1 litre of aquafaba, for the same price of a tin, and with a better quality than the jar... If you don't need the aquafaba straight away, it's definitely the best way.

What next?

Obtaining the aquafaba is one thing, preserving it is another. Just because we're cooking chickpeas or opening a tin, it doesn't necessarily mean that we'll be needing vegan egg whites straight away. However, now we know the incredible properties of this leftover liquid, we can't just throw it away!

Aquafaba keeps well in the fridge for a good week. You just have to make sure to keep it in a tightly sealed glass jar or bottle. It may become decanted with a clear liquid rising to the top and a cloudy substance at the bottom, but don't worry, it's normal. Just shake the contents before using them and the two parts will merge.

Another method is simply to freeze it. You can fill ice cube trays with aquafaba: a practical way to split the liquid into portions. In this way it can be kept in the freezer for several months. You can unfreeze it slowly at room temperature or, if you're in a rush, in a bain-marie.

HOME-MADE
AQUAFABA

There's nothing easier than making home-made aquafaba yourself. You just need to be prepared.

Rinse 500 g dried chickpeas in cold water to remove any dust and tiny impurities.
Cover the chickpeas with a generous layer of water in a large bowl. Make sure that it's large enough: the chickpeas will swell to double their volume. Soak for 12 hours.
Next, discard the soaking water, rinse the chickpeas again and move on to the cooking process.

There are two ways to cook the rehydrated chickpeas:

In a pressure cooker: Immerse the rehydrated chickpeas in 3 litres of water. Cook for 40 minutes at high pressure.

In a saucepan: Bring 3 litres of water to the boil and add the rehydrated chickpeas. Once it comes to the boil again, simmer for 90 minutes.

Whichever method you choose, make sure not to add salt to ensure that the aquafaba remains as neutral as possible. Once the chickpeas are drained you should have 1 litre of raw aquafaba. But we're not finished yet! We have to reduce the liquid by a quarter to make the proteins and nutrients more concentrated. In order to do so, pour the liquid into a saucepan, bring it to the boil, then reduce the heat to low. Leave it to simmer for 10 minutes to evaporate a quarter of the liquid. You should check the level of reduction regularly in a measuring jug. So, 1 litre of raw aquafaba should yield 750 ml of reduced aquafaba.

If you have time, it is a good idea to keep the aquafaba in direct contact with the cooked chickpeas for 48 hours. In other words, fill a glass jar with the chickpeas, pour the aquafaba over the top, then close the jar tightly and keep it in the fridge. By doing so, you can obtain a thicker, richer aquafaba, with a viscous texture... just like egg whites. If, on the other hand, you are in a rush, you can always fall back on using tinned or jarred chickpeas. You just have to remember to reduce the drained liquid as explained.

USEFUL EQUIPMENT

Stand mixer
This is the essential machine for any true pâtisserie enthusiasts. There's no doubt about it, using a stand mixer is the most practical and easiest way to turn your aquafaba into soft peaks. You can control the whisking without even using your hands, leaving you free to prepare other parts of the recipe while the machine does all the work for you, thereby saving you both time and energy.

Electric whisk

A simple electric whisk also gives you a good result. It's just a bit more tiring, because you have to use your wrist to guide the rotations of the whisk in the bowl throughout the preparation process. However, an electric whisk does have one huge advantage: you can whisk small amounts. In fact, when using a stand mixer you need at least 80 ml aquafaba, while if you're using an electric whisk there is no minimum requirement.

Hand blender

You may be more familiar with using it to make simple soups, but did you know that hand blenders can also be used to emulsify your dishes and to prevent lumps from forming in creams. Some hand blenders are even equipped with special attachments for whisking egg whites. You may not get such a good result as when using a stand mixer or an electric whisk and it won't create stiff peaks, but it can be used to make a good froth.

Scales

As always, we cannot stress enough the importance of using the measurements as stated in the recipes. This means that a precise set of weighing scales is an indispensable piece of equipment. We would recommend digital scales that are accurate to 1 mg. Unfortunately, it's quite difficult to get hold of these and they can be fairly expensive. If you have a standard set of scales, it will probably only start reacting over 5 g weight. Here is our trick: put a small bowl on the scales, take note of the weight, then add the ingredient to reach the desired amount. However for those without digital scales there are conversions for smaller weights of ingredients.

Measuring spoons

In some countries an imperial measuring system that is based on volume rather than weight is used. This is where measuring spoons and cups originated from. If you're using a metric system, these may seem useless, but, they actually come in very handy for measuring small quantities of liquid. Here is how to convert the measurements:
• 1 tablespoon = 15 ml • 1 teaspoon = 5 ml • ½ teaspoon = 2.5 ml
• ¼ teaspoon = 1.25 ml • ⅛ teaspoon = 0.625 ml.

SAVOURY
RECIPES

TOMATO AND BASIL
MOUSSE

This light, gourmet starter with its Mediterranean flavours is the epitome of the spirit of summer. Just imagine that we've replaced the traditional chocolate with sun-dried tomatoes to get an idea of the texture that awaits you.

SERVES **2** - PREPARATION TIME: **15 MINUTES**

INGREDIENTS • 90 ml aquafaba • 2.5 ml cider vinegar • 1 g (⅓ tsp) cream of tartar • 60 ml soya cream • 100 g sun-dried tomatoes in oil • 1 pinch Espelette pepper • 10 g fresh basil • 60 ml white wine • 60 ml plain soya milk • 2 g (1 tsp) sweet paprika • 1 pinch fine salt • 2 g (½ tsp) agar-agar

Method: Pour the aquafaba, vinegar and cream of tartar into the stand mixer. Whisk at full power until soft peaks have formed. In the meantime, place the soya cream, lightly drained sun-dried tomatoes and Espelette pepper in a bowl and finely blend using a hand blender. Add the fresh basil, chopped, and mix one last time. Set aside. Whisk the white wine, soya milk, paprika and salt together in a small saucepan and heat. Once it begins to boil, sprinkle in the agar-agar and boil for 2 minutes, whisking continuously. Pour the liquid immediately over the sun-dried tomatoes mixture and incorporate with a hand blender. Transfer into a mixing bowl. Turn off the stand mixer, add the soft peaks of the aquafaba to the bowl and gently fold in using a spatula, making sure to stir in the same direction, until the mixture forms a mousse. Distribute the mixture between the small verrines and refrigerate for a few hours. Sprinkle a couple of pinches of Espelette pepper on top and add a basil garnish. Serve with breadsticks or some puff pastry twists.

Comments: If you are in a rush and want to make this recipe at the last minute, just put the verrines in the freezer for 15 minutes. They can then be served straight away.

SCANDINAVIAN **VERRINES**

Here again, aquafaba gives you a delicate cream-like texture. Using a little imagination, you can even infuse it with aromas to give it a surprising taste. This verrine, although not a traditional recipe, is inspired by the distinctive flavours of Scandinavia.

MAKES **4** VERRINES - PREPARATION TIME: **15 MINUTES**

INGREDIENTS • 1 medium carrot • Lemon juice • 1 cucumber • 10 g dill • 5 g (1½ tsp) mixed seaweed flakes • 3 g (1 tsp) pink peppercorns • 2 g (⅓ tsp) fine salt • 5 g (1 tsp) caster sugar • Cider vinegar • 10 ml olive oil • 60 ml aquafaba • 1 g (¼ tsp) guar gum • 50 ml lacto-fermented thick soya cream • 2 ml (½ tsp) liquid smoke

Method: Peel the carrot and create fine ribbons using a vegetable peeler. Transfer into a bowl, add a dash of lemon juice, combine and set aside. Wash the cucumber, cut off the ends and cut into small dice (approximately 1 cm). Transfer the cucumber dice into a bowl and mix with the coarsely chopped dill, seaweed flakes and pink peppercorns, lightly crushed with a pestle. In a small bowl, mix salt and sugar, add 10 ml vinegar, olive oil and 10 ml cold water. Mix well until the sugar has dissolved. Pour this seasoning over the cucumber dice and let stand while you prepare the cream.
Pour the aquafaba, guar gum and 3 ml cider vinegar into the stand mixer. Whisk at full power until soft peaks have formed. In the meantime, mix the soya cream with the liquid smoke and a pinch of salt. Once dense aquafaba peaks have formed, set the mixer to the lowest speed and add the smoked cream to incorporate the whole mixture.
Assembly: Distribute the cucumber dice equally between 4 verrines, add the carrot ribbons and finish with the smoked cream. Garnish with a sprig of dill and some pink peppercorns. Serve immediately.

Comments: This starter is best enjoyed chilled, for this reason we recommend keeping all of the ingredients refrigerated before use. Also, it should be eaten immediately after preparation. Otherwise, the cream will subside and the vegetables will soften due to the acidity.

DEVIL'S
MAYONNAISE

Often aquafaba is used to create soft peaks. However, its natural properties also lend it to other purposes. For example, it can be emulsified with fat to obtain a mayonnaise-like texture. Also, by adding a pinch of Kala Namak Himalayan black salt, we can even obtain a flavour and odour that is disconcertingly close to that of eggs. You'll be amazed!

MAKES A POT OF **370 ML** - PREPARATION TIME: **5 MINUTES**

INGREDIENTS • 50 ml aquafaba • 15 ml cider vinegar • 5 g (1 tsp) Dijon mustard • 2 g (⅓ tsp) Kala Namak salt • 200 ml rapeseed oil • 10 g (2 tsp) tomato purée • 2 g (1 tsp) Espelette pepper • 1 small garlic clove

Method: You will need a hand blender and its beaker. Put the aquafaba, cider vinegar, mustard and Kala Namak salt into the beaker. Blend at full power until you obtain a frothy and consistent mixture. Gradually drizzle in the oil, while continuing to blend.
The thickening process takes some time: a good 5 minutes are needed for the emulsion to start solidifying. When it does, add the tomato purée, Espelette pepper and garlic clove, pressed.

Blend one last time for 1 minute to incorporate the mixture. Refrigerate for at least 1 hour before serving.

Comments: This mayonnaise recipe can be customised at will. You can substitute the tomato, pepper and garlic for other similar ingredients to suit your taste. Or, why not make a more classical mayonnaise by leaving it plain.

SAFFRON
TAGLIATELLE

Pasta has been a staple food for many people throughout history. Its simple and nourishing characteristics are extremely popular. Unfortunately, the fresh pasta that we can find in shops almost always contains egg. But now it's easy to make your own 100% vegan fresh pasta using aquafaba. This precious liquid provides a great elasticity. The result is impressive and easily rivals fresh egg pasta.

MAKES **600 G** - PREPARATION TIME: **30 MIN.** - RESTING TIME: **15 MIN.** - COOKING TIME: **3 MIN.**

INGREDIENTS • 0.5 g saffron • 150 g soft white flour • 250 g fine durum wheat semolina • 1 g (⅓ tsp) Kala Namak salt • 90 ml aquafaba

Method: Infuse the saffron in 5 ml cold water. Combine the flour, durum wheat semolina and salt in a mixing bowl. Add the aquafaba and knead by hand. Next, add the saffron infused water and 100 ml water. Knead again until a firm dough is formed. Place the dough on a floured work surface and work with the palm of your hand, folding it over upon itself. Repeat this process around a dozen times to soften the dough. Divide the dough into four and flatten each piece. One at a time, pass the pieces through a pasta rolling machine, set at number 2. Fold the rolled strip over upon itself and repeat the process three times. Next, set the rolling machine to number 5 and repeat the process. In total, the pastry should have passed through the machine six times. Place the long strips of pasta on a generously floured work surface and lightly sprinkle with flour. Set the machine to the tagliatelle setting, pass a strip of pasta through it and hang the cut tagliatelle straight over a pasta drying rack. Repeat the process, using up all of the dough and leave the tagliatelle to dry in the open air for at least 15 minutes. Cooking: Bring a large pan of water to the boil, adding 1 tbsp coarse salt per litre. Once it boils, immerse the pasta in the water, stir gently to make sure that they don't stick together and simmer for 3 minutes. Drain, season and serve.

LITTLE BURGER
BUNS

———

A good burger is made up of three key elements that can make all the difference. A good filling, a tasty sauce and high quality bread. For the bread, nothing beats home-made buns, eaten fresh for unrivalled taste. Here, we can use aquafaba to replace the binding properties of egg whites and also to stick seeds on top of the buns.

———

MAKES **4–6** BUNS - PREPARATION TIME: **15 MINUTES** - RESTING TIME: **1 HOUR 30 MINUTES**

INGREDIENTS • 10 g (1 tbsp) fresh yeast • 15 g (1 tbsp) cane sugar • 120 ml plain soya milk • 30 ml rapeseed oil • 50 ml aquafaba • 6 g (1 tsp) fine salt • 400 g soft wheat flour • 5 g (1 tsp) sesame seeds • 5 g (1 tsp) blue poppy seeds

Method: In a small bowl, dissolve the fresh yeast in 100 ml lukewarm water. Once it has dissolved, add the sugar and mix. Pour into the stand mixer with a bread hook attached. Add the soya milk, oil, aquafaba and salt. Beat for a few seconds, then add the flour. Set to knead at ⅔ power for a good 5 minutes to form the bread dough. Place the dough in a generously floured mixing bowl, cover with a damp cloth and let rise in a warm place for 1 hour. Once the time is up and the dough has risen, knead lightly and divide either into four for large buns, or six for medium-sized buns. Shape the dough into balls using the floured palm of your hand. Place them on a baking tray lined with baking paper or a baking mat. Let them rise for 30 minutes in a warm place. Preheat the oven for a few minutes at 190°C/375°F/gas 5. Brush the buns with aquafaba, sprinkle with poppy and sesame seeds and bake for 15 minutes. Leave to cool slightly before serving.

Comments: To get your dough to rise, you can also place the bowl with the dough, without the cloth, in a previously warmed oven. Better still, if you have a bread proofer, you can use it set at 30°C/86°F. In both cases, allow your dough to rise for 1 hour, then 30 minutes after shaping.

CAPPUCCINO
SOUP

———

The famous cappuccino is a truly comforting drink with its strong coffee taste paired with smooth milk. This was the inspiration for this recipe in which aquafaba plays the important role of creating a mousse that is both dense and light. Coffee isn't something you'd usually associate with savoury dishes. However, it works surprisingly well!

———

SERVES **4** - PREPARATION TIME: **20 MINUTES** - COOKING TIME: **5–10 MINUTES**

INGREDIENTS • 600 g cooked chickpeas • Olive oil • 1 garlic clove • 3 g (1 tsp) cumin seeds • 1 litre vegetable stock • 3 g (1 tsp) Ras el Hanout • 80 ml espresso (medium roast) • 50 ml aquafaba • 5 ml balsamic vinegar • Black pepper • Fine salt

Method: Fry the chickpeas with a dash of olive oil, the peeled and crushed garlic clove and cumin seeds. Add 2 g salt and cook over a medium heat for 5 minutes.
Prepare 1 litre of piping hot vegetable stock. Combine the chickpeas, vegetable stock and Ras el Hanout and blend until you get a velouté. Lastly, add the coffee and blend briefly.
Pour the aquafaba, balsamic vinegar, pepper and salt into the stand mixer. Whisk at full power for 5 minutes.
The mousse is now ready to be used.
Pour the chickpea soup into a mug, add a generous layer of mousse and serve immediately, before it cools.

Comments: If you prepare this recipe in advance, add the coffee at the end, just before serving. The coffee must not be reheated because it would make the soup too bitter. The mousse should be prepared and served quickly, otherwise it will lose its smooth and dense texture.

BEER **BATTER**

The main ingredient of this traditional coating may come as a surprise: beer! However, it's this very ingredient that makes this light batter hold together so well. Here once more, we can use the flexible properties of aquafaba to replace the egg whites.

SERVES **4** - PREPARATION TIME: **20 MINUTES** - COOKING TIME: **15 MINUTES**

INGREDIENTS • 3 slices textured soya protein (big steak) • 1 litre vegetable stock • 3 bay leaves • 2 sprigs thyme • 150 g soft wheat flour • 2 g (⅓ tsp) fine salt • 2 g (1 tsp) turmeric • 50 ml aquafaba • 200 ml beer (pale ale or lager)

Method: Cook the textured soya slices in a saucepan for 10 minutes with 1 litre vegetable stock, bay leaves and thyme. Once they are cooked, drain and press well to extract as much liquid as possible. Leave to cool.

In the meantime, place the flour, fine salt, turmeric, aquafaba and beer in a mixing bowl. Mix well using a whisk to obtain a smooth batter with no lumps. Let stand for 30 minutes.

Heat a deep fryer filled with vegetable oil to 180 °C. Cut the textured soya protein lengthways, at a slight angle.

Dip each piece, one by one, into the batter, allowing the excess to drain off and place in the deep fryer. Deep-fry for 2 minutes and drain on a paper towel.

Serve with some chips and a sauce of your choice.

Comments: For this recipe, we have used textured soya, but it is also possible to use other ingredients to experiment with textures and flavours. It would work well, for example, with a slice of seitan, herbed tofu or even blanched cauliflower.

FORAGER'S
MILLE-FEUILLES

This recipe is very versatile. It can be served hot or cold, depending on the season and your preferences. It can also be served as a starter or a main course, it's entirely up to you.

SERVES **2** - PREPARATION TIME: **20 MINUTES** - COOKING TIME: **20 MINUTES**

INGREDIENTS • 1 pack pre-rolled vegan puff pastry • 6 shallots • 50 ml white wine • 10 g flat-leaf parsley • 350 g button mushrooms • 1 garlic clove • 2 cloves • 15 ml Jägermeister • 50 ml aquafaba • 5 ml cider vinegar • 2 g (½ tsp) cream of tartar • Pinch grated nutmeg • Pinch garlic powder • Olive oil • Black pepper • Fine salt

Method: Preheat the oven to 180°C/350°F/gas 4 and bake the puff pastry blind for 20 minutes, placing it between 2 baking sheets to make sure it stays flat. Leave to cool and cut into 4 equally sized squares. Meanwhile, finely chop the shallots and brown in a saucepan with a dash of olive oil. Once they become translucent, add salt and deglaze with white wine. Reduce on a very low heat until they become soft. Chop the parsley, add to the cooked shallots, and then set aside. Wash and quarter the mushrooms. Fry with a crushed garlic clove and a little olive oil. Add the cloves, season and leave to reduce. Once the mushrooms start to brown, deglaze with Jägermeister. Cook until the liquid has completely evaporated. Once cooked, finely chop the mushrooms. Place the aquafaba, vinegar, cream of tartar and a pinch of salt in the stand mixer. Whisk at full power for 10 minutes to obtain a dense and firm mousse. After 5 minutes, add the nutmeg and garlic powder. Use the mousse to fill a pastry bag with a Saint Honoré decorating tip. Assembly: Using a square of puff pastry as a base, add a layer of mushrooms, press down firmly and add the shallots. Cover with another square of puff pastry and finish off with the mousse, piped in zigzags. Sprinkle with a few pinches of Espelette or black pepper. Serve quickly as the mousse is fragile.

BASIL PESTO
MUFFINS

We've all enjoyed a rich chocolate muffin with a nice cup of coffee... so why not try out a savoury version? It could accompany a glass of wine for an apéritif, a hearty soup or even a family picnic. These muffins will turn any of these occasions into a real treat.

MAKES **6** MUFFINS - PREPARATION TIME: **15 MINUTES** - COOKING TIME: **20 MINUTES**

INGREDIENTS • 120 ml aquafaba • 80 g white almond butter • 200 g strong bread flour • 10 g (2 tsp) baking powder • 20 g fresh basil • 40 g cashew nuts • 5 g fresh garlic • 100 ml olive oil • Unrefined fine salt • Pepper • 5 g (1½ tsp) nutritional yeast • 45 ml soya milk

Method: Preheat the oven to 180°C/350°F/gas 4. Mix the aquafaba with the white almond butter in a large bowl and set aside. In a separate bowl, combine the flour with the baking powder. Finely chop the basil leaves, grind the cashew nuts to make a powder and press a garlic clove. Put the oil, nutritional yeast, garlic and basil in the hand blender beaker and season to your taste. Blend for 2 minutes, then add the cashew nut powder and blend again for 1 minute. Pour this mixture over the aquafaba/almond purée mixture, combine, and pour over the flour. Whisk vigorously. The mixture will be very thick; thin it down with soya milk and mix once again. Line a muffin tin with 6 paper muffin cases and fill, using an ice-cream scoop.
The cases should be ¾ full. Bake for 20 minutes without opening the oven. Allow to cool before removing from the tin.

Comments: These muffins taste even better the following day. Just leave them to dry in the open air, if you have the patience! However, do not leave for longer than 48 hours.

CUMIN
CRACKERS

Aquafaba isn't just used in the form of soft peaks. We can also use it as a binder, just like unbeaten egg whites. Find out how in this recipe. These crackers are very easy and quick to make as well as being delicious and dangerously addictive.

MAKES **10–12** CRACKERS - PREPARATION TIME: **5 MINUTES** - COOKING TIME: **12 MINUTES**

INGREDIENTS • 50 g strong bread flour • 50 ml aquafaba • 40 g dairy-free butter • 5 g (1 tsp) cumin seeds • 5 g (1½ tsp) nutritional yeast • Unrefined fine salt • Freshly ground pepper

Method: Preheat the oven to 180°C/350°F/gas 4.
Next, roast the cumin seeds in a very hot frying pan without oil or fat for 30 seconds. Leave to cool on a small plate.
In a large bowl, combine the flour and aquafaba. Then add the dairy-free butter, slightly softened, and mix well with a spoon to obtain a smooth mixture. Add the cumin seeds and nutritional yeast, season to suit your taste, then mix one last time.
On a baking tray covered with baking paper, gently spread the mixture using a spatula. Use the equivalent of 1 tsp per cracker, at a thickness of barely 1mm. Bake for 12 minutes and leave to cool completely before serving.

Comments: Depending on whether you use a gas or electric oven, cooking times may vary. You should check on the crackers after 7 minutes to see whether they are golden or not. Here is a little tip to get crackers of an identical size and thickness: cut out circles in a plastic place mat and then use as moulds when you're spreading the mixture. All you have to do is draw a spatula across the surface to remove the surplus. This will give you completely even, one-millimetre-thick crackers.

SWEET
RECIPES

ALMOND
MERINGUES

Meringues come in many different flavours, shapes and forms. But one of the most emblematic is the kind you find in bakery windows: a vanilla-flavoured, white meringue, sprinkled with grilled almonds. The taste will put you up on cloud nine!

MAKES **7** MERINGUES - PREPARATION TIME: **10 MINUTES** - COOKING TIME: **1 HOUR 15 MINUTES**

INGREDIENTS • 100 ml aquafaba • 3 ml lemon juice • 5 ml vanilla extract • 200 g icing sugar • 4 g (1 tsp) cream of tartar • Flaked almonds

Method: Preheat the oven to 120°C/250°F/gas ½. Move the oven shelf to the bottom of the oven. Pour the aquafaba, lemon juice and vanilla extract into the stand mixer and whisk at full power for 5 minutes. Meanwhile, mix the icing sugar with the cream of tartar, and sieve to remove any lumps of sugar.

Once the aquafaba mixture has formed stiff peaks, add the icing sugar mixture gradually, whisking for a further 3 minutes. The meringue mixture is ready to use when it doesn't fall easily from the whisk. Use the mixture to fill a pastry bag with a star-shaped nozzle. Pipe out equally sized meringues on a baking tray covered with baking paper.

Sprinkle some almond flakes on top, pressing lightly to embed them and bake for 1 hour 15 minutes without opening the oven. Leave to cool completely and store in a dry place for a half or whole day before serving.

Comments: The meringues can be kept for a few days in a dry place and in the open air.

ÎLES **FLOTTANTES**

This is one of the emblematic desserts of Parisian brasseries, standing proudly beside chocolate mousses and lemon meringue pies.
A nostalgic treat and truly one of the greats.

SERVES **4** - PREPARATION TIME: **15–20 MINUTES** - COOKING TIME: **8 MINUTES**

INGREDIENTS • 500 ml soya milk • 1 vanilla pod • 15 g cornflour
• 165 g caster sugar • 1 pinch turmeric • 95 ml aquafaba • ½ tsp vanilla extract
• 70 g icing sugar • 2 g (⅔ tsp) cream of tartar • Flaked almonds

Method: First, pour the soya milk into a small saucepan, split the vanilla pod, remove the seeds and infuse everything (including the pod) over a medium heat. Once it boils, remove from the heat. Place the cornflour, 90 g of sugar and pinch of turmeric in a bowl. Add the hot milk, removing the vanilla pod and mix vigorously. Pour this mixture into the saucepan. Cook over a medium heat, whisking regularly, for a few minutes allowing it to thicken. Remove from heat and leave to cool Preheat the oven to 180°C/350°F/gas 4. Place 4 baking rings (8 cm diameter) on a baking tray covered with baking paper. Using a brush, grease the insides of the rings with vegetable oil. Pour the aquafaba and vanilla extract into the stand mixer and whisk at full power until the mixture forms stiff peaks. Gradually add the icing sugar and the cream of tartar, and whisk for a further 3 minutes at full power. Fill the rings to the brim with the stiff peaks of the aquafaba mixture and smooth the tops with a spoon to ensure there are no air bubbles. Bake for 8 minutes. Remove from the oven, leave to cool and refrigerate for 2 hours. Just before serving, make the caramel decoration. Heat 75 g sugar with 25 ml water in a small saucepan, over a medium heat without stirring. Remove from the heat once it turns a light, amber colour and stop the cooking process by placing the saucepan in a sink filled with cold water. Wait a few minutes until the caramel starts to solidify and then use a spoon to create caramel shards on a sheet of baking paper by 'painting' wave forms. Serve the baked aquafaba peaks in 4 bowls, pouring the cold crème anglaise around them, decorate with the caramel and finish off with a few flaked almonds.

CHOCOLATE **MOUSSE**

There are numerous chocolate mousse recipes for vegans. However, for many the name is merely symbolic. The reason is that whisked egg whites are the key ingredient for making this dessert with its unique texture: it was foolish to think we could get the same texture using silken tofu. Luckily, aquafaba has arrived and has revolutionised everything!

SERVES **2–4** - PREPARATION TIME: **15 MINUTES** - RESTING TIME: **3 HOURS**

INGREDIENTS • 200 g dark chocolate (74% cocoa maximum) • ½ tonka bean • 200 ml aquafaba • 5 ml cider vinegar • 100 g icing sugar

Method: Melt the chocolate in a bain-marie over a very low heat, grate the tonka bean over the top and incorporate.
Once the chocolate is partially melted, remove from the heat and allow to melt slowly, stirring occasionally.
Meanwhile, pour the aquafaba and vinegar into the stand mixer. Whisk at full power until the liquid forms soft peaks. Sprinkle in the icing sugar, continuing to whisk. The mixture should form stiff peaks. Whisk for 10 minutes.

Stop the stand mixer, remove the whisk and pour the melted chocolate over the stiff peaks. Gently fold the two mixtures together, using a spatula and taking care to stir in the same direction lifting the peaks so that they don't disintegrate.
Once you have made the mousse, distribute into serving glasses and refrigerate for 3 hours.

Serve with vegan chantilly cream and some chocolate grated over the top.

Comments: This mousse can be kept for 48 hours in the fridge.

NANCY
MACARONS

Everyone knows that the Parisian macaron is made of two meringue cookies sandwiched together with ganache or cream. But did you know that before this type, there were many different traditional macarons, which varied from region to region? One of the most emblematic types is a macaron from Nancy, a particularly tasty speciality from the region of Lorraine. The original recipe has remained a well-guarded secret since the 18th century, but it's not too difficult to hazard a guess at it.

MAKES **16—18** UNITS - PREPARATION TIME: **5 MINUTES** - COOKING TIME: **25 MINUTES**

INGREDIENTS • 160 g ground almonds • 120 g granulated sugar • 50 g strong bread flour • 80 ml aquafaba • 10 ml vanilla extract • 1 pinch salt • Icing sugar

Method: Preheat the oven to 160°C/325°F/gas 3. Place the ground almonds, granulated sugar and flour in an appropriately sized bowl and mix well. Pour the aquafaba, vanilla extract and salt into the stand mixer. Whisk the mixture until the aquafaba becomes frothy and thick, but still hasn't formed peaks. Pour this mixture over the dry mixture and fold using a spatula, pressing against the sides. Tip the icing sugar into a bowl, make small walnut-sized balls of the mixture and roll in the icing sugar. Place the balls on a baking tray covered with baking paper and bake for 15 minutes. Once this time is up, raise the temperature to 180°C/350°F/gas 4 and cook for a further 10 minutes. Leave to cool in the oven with the door ajar and serve when cool. The macarons can be kept in an airtight container for several days.

Comments: Use the aquafaba at room temperature. After the first baking, if the macarons haven't spread and cracked a little, flatten slightly with your fingers before the second baking to encourage the cracking process.

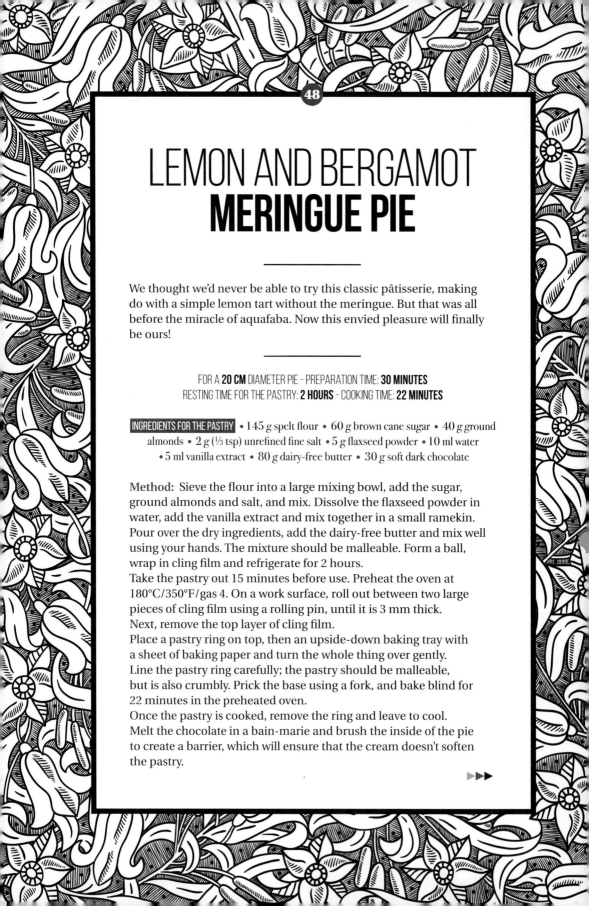

LEMON AND BERGAMOT
MERINGUE PIE

———————

We thought we'd never be able to try this classic pâtisserie, making do with a simple lemon tart without the meringue. But that was all before the miracle of aquafaba. Now this envied pleasure will finally be ours!

———————

FOR A **20 CM** DIAMETER PIE - PREPARATION TIME: **30 MINUTES**
RESTING TIME FOR THE PASTRY: **2 HOURS** - COOKING TIME: **22 MINUTES**

INGREDIENTS FOR THE PASTRY • 145 g spelt flour • 60 g brown cane sugar • 40 g ground almonds • 2 g (⅓ tsp) unrefined fine salt • 5 g flaxseed powder • 10 ml water • 5 ml vanilla extract • 80 g dairy-free butter • 30 g soft dark chocolate

Method: Sieve the flour into a large mixing bowl, add the sugar, ground almonds and salt, and mix. Dissolve the flaxseed powder in water, add the vanilla extract and mix together in a small ramekin. Pour over the dry ingredients, add the dairy-free butter and mix well using your hands. The mixture should be malleable. Form a ball, wrap in cling film and refrigerate for 2 hours.
Take the pastry out 15 minutes before use. Preheat the oven at 180°C/350°F/gas 4. On a work surface, roll out between two large pieces of cling film using a rolling pin, until it is 3 mm thick.
Next, remove the top layer of cling film.
Place a pastry ring on top, then an upside-down baking tray with a sheet of baking paper and turn the whole thing over gently.
Line the pastry ring carefully; the pastry should be malleable, but is also crumbly. Prick the base using a fork, and bake blind for 22 minutes in the preheated oven.
Once the pastry is cooked, remove the ring and leave to cool.
Melt the chocolate in a bain-marie and brush the inside of the pie to create a barrier, which will ensure that the cream doesn't soften the pastry.

▶▶▶

LEMON AND BERGAMOT **MERINGUE PIE**

—————

INGREDIENTS FOR THE LEMON CREAM • 200 ml lemon juice • 100 ml water • 10 drops bergamot essential oil • 60 g cornflour • 280 g cane sugar • 30 g bergamot zest • 100 ml liquid soya cream • 40 g dairy-free butter

Method: Pour the lemon juice, water, essential oil, cornflour and sugar into a small saucepan and mix to dissolve. Add the bergamot zest. Cook over a medium heat, stirring continuously. When the sauce thickens, leave to boil for a few seconds longer, then remove from the heat. Add the soya cream, whisk well and then add the dairy-free butter, whisking again. Pour over the base of the pie and refrigerate for 1 hour.

INGREDIENTS FOR THE MERINGUE • 100 ml aquafaba • 3 g (1 tsp) cream of tartar • 3 ml cider vinegar • 5 ml vanilla extract • 200 g icing sugar

Method: Pour the aquafaba, cream of tartar, vinegar and vanilla extract into the stand mixer. Whisk at full power for 5 minutes. Meanwhile, sieve the icing sugar. When the aquafaba has formed stiff peaks, gradually add the icing sugar and whisk at full power for a few more minutes.
Now you can spread the meringue over the lemon cream.

Caramelise the top of the meringue using a blow torch. Refrigerate until serving.

Comments: This pie can be kept for 2 days in the fridge.

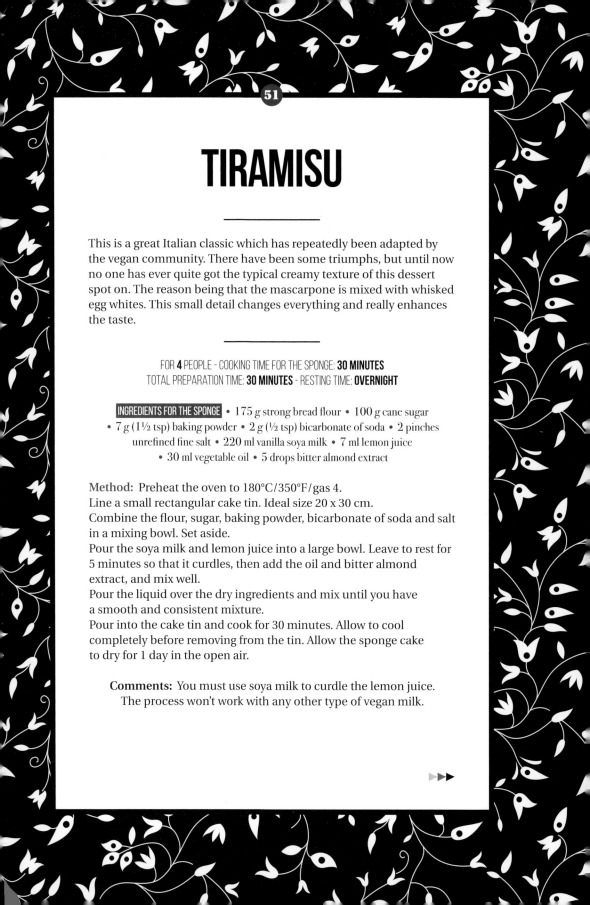

TIRAMISU

This is a great Italian classic which has repeatedly been adapted by the vegan community. There have been some triumphs, but until now no one has ever quite got the typical creamy texture of this dessert spot on. The reason being that the mascarpone is mixed with whisked egg whites. This small detail changes everything and really enhances the taste.

FOR **4** PEOPLE - COOKING TIME FOR THE SPONGE: **30 MINUTES**
TOTAL PREPARATION TIME: **30 MINUTES** - RESTING TIME: **OVERNIGHT**

INGREDIENTS FOR THE SPONGE • 175 g strong bread flour • 100 g cane sugar • 7 g (1½ tsp) baking powder • 2 g (½ tsp) bicarbonate of soda • 2 pinches unrefined fine salt • 220 ml vanilla soya milk • 7 ml lemon juice • 30 ml vegetable oil • 5 drops bitter almond extract

Method: Preheat the oven to 180°C/350°F/gas 4.
Line a small rectangular cake tin. Ideal size 20 x 30 cm.
Combine the flour, sugar, baking powder, bicarbonate of soda and salt in a mixing bowl. Set aside.
Pour the soya milk and lemon juice into a large bowl. Leave to rest for 5 minutes so that it curdles, then add the oil and bitter almond extract, and mix well.
Pour the liquid over the dry ingredients and mix until you have a smooth and consistent mixture.
Pour into the cake tin and cook for 30 minutes. Allow to cool completely before removing from the tin. Allow the sponge cake to dry for 1 day in the open air.

Comments: You must use soya milk to curdle the lemon juice. The process won't work with any other type of vegan milk.

▶▶▶

TIRAMISU

INGREDIENTS FOR THE CREAM • 50 g white almond butter • 100 g cane sugar
• 30 ml soya milk • Vanilla extract • 235 ml lacto-fermented thick
soya cream • 80 ml aquafaba • 2.5 ml cider vinegar • 2 g (⅔ tsp) cream of tartar
• 80 g icing sugar • 200 ml strong coffee • 40 ml Amaretto

Method: Mix the almond butter vigorously with the sugar in a mixing
bowl, add the soya milk and 15 ml vanilla extract. The sugar should
have dissolved and the mixture should be smooth. Next, add the thick
cream and mix one last time. Set aside.
Pour the aquafaba, cider vinegar and cream of tartar into the stand
mixer and whisk at full power. When the mixture starts to form soft
peaks add another 2.5 ml vanilla extract. Without stopping the mixer,
add the icing sugar gradually and allow the peaks to form for
5 minutes. The peaks should be stiff and should stick to the whisk.
Pour the stiff peaks over the previous mixture and gently fold using
a spatula, making sure to stir in the same direction. Set aside.

Pour the strong coffee and Amaretto into a small bowl, cut the sponge
cake into batons 2 cm by 10 cm to get 18 pieces. Soak the pieces of
sponge cake generously in the liquid and line the bottom of
a ramekin, add a 2 cm layer of the cream, another layer of soaked
sponge and, lastly, another layer of cream. Repeat for the other
ramekins. Sprinkle with cocoa powder and keep in the open air
overnight.

Comments: Alternatively, you can make a large tiramisu. If you do so,
there is no need to cut the sponge into small pieces, you can just cut it
into two. Keeps for 2 days maximum in the fridge.

FRENCH **TOAST**

What can you do with leftover bread from the previous day?
You could always toast it for breakfast, but true food lovers will tell
you it's the perfect excuse to make French toast! It's a very simple
recipe to make and only needs a few ingredients. We use the binding
qualities of aquafaba to replace the egg whites.

MAKES **6** SLICES - PREPARATION TIME: **10 MINUTES** - COOKING TIME: **6 MINUTES**

INGREDIENTS • 1 loaf of bread (one day old) • 300 ml soya milk
• 15 g vanilla sugar • 40 g sugar • 60 ml aquafaba
• 1 vanilla pod • Dairy-free butter

Method: Cut 6 slices of bread, the slices should be around 2 cm thick.
Mix the soya milk, two types of sugar and aquafaba in a bowl. Split
the vanilla pod lengthways and remove the seeds with a knife.
Add the seeds to the liquid and whisk until everything is incorpora-
ted. Pour the liquid into a large dish and soak the 6 slices of bread for
5 to 10 minutes according to the state of the bread (stale to dry). Heat
a knob of butter in a frying pan until it becomes frothy. Press the
soaked slices of bread lightly to remove the excess liquid. Just enough
so that they don't drip when you pick them up. Place the slices in
a frying pan and brown for 3 minutes on each side. Serve with fresh
fruit and a little caramel for anyone with an extra sweet tooth.

Comments: Of course, the way in which this recipe turns out will
depend on the type of bread you use. Here, we used a country loaf
that had been kept in the open air for 48 hours.
You should preferably use a hard-crusted, light bread to obtain
the best results. With sandwich bread, the effect is a lot softer,
but still delicious.

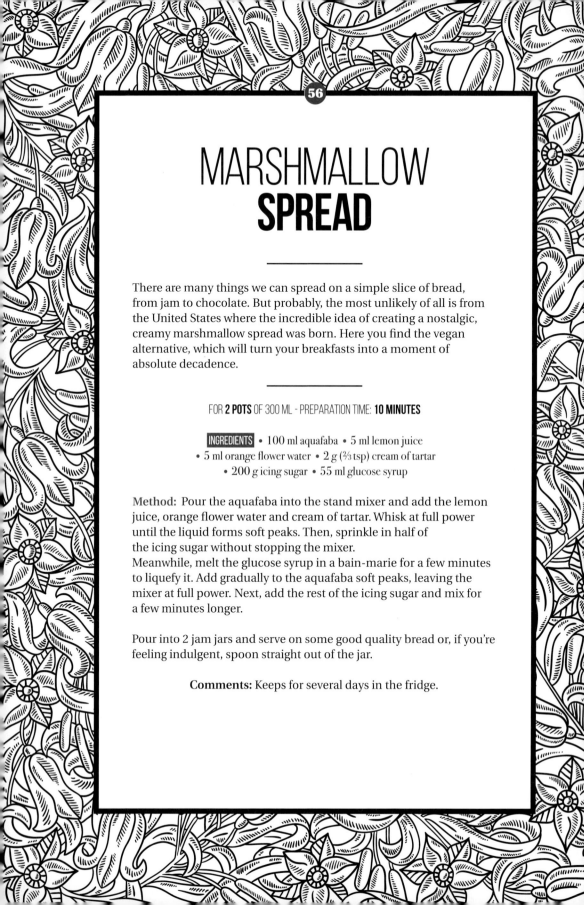

MARSHMALLOW
SPREAD

There are many things we can spread on a simple slice of bread, from jam to chocolate. But probably, the most unlikely of all is from the United States where the incredible idea of creating a nostalgic, creamy marshmallow spread was born. Here you find the vegan alternative, which will turn your breakfasts into a moment of absolute decadence.

FOR **2 POTS** OF 300 ML - PREPARATION TIME: **10 MINUTES**

INGREDIENTS • 100 ml aquafaba • 5 ml lemon juice
• 5 ml orange flower water • 2 g (⅔ tsp) cream of tartar
• 200 g icing sugar • 55 ml glucose syrup

Method: Pour the aquafaba into the stand mixer and add the lemon juice, orange flower water and cream of tartar. Whisk at full power until the liquid forms soft peaks. Then, sprinkle in half of the icing sugar without stopping the mixer.
Meanwhile, melt the glucose syrup in a bain-marie for a few minutes to liquefy it. Add gradually to the aquafaba soft peaks, leaving the mixer at full power. Next, add the rest of the icing sugar and mix for a few minutes longer.

Pour into 2 jam jars and serve on some good quality bread or, if you're feeling indulgent, spoon straight out of the jar.

Comments: Keeps for several days in the fridge.

AMARENA CHERRY
PAVLOVA

———

Contrary to popular belief, this dessert isn't from Russia, but actually arrived from New Zealand. It was named after a Russian ballerina from the early 20th century, Anna Pavlova. It consists of a meringue base topped with whipped cream and fruit. It can be customised as much as you like, which is exactly what we've done.

———

MAKES **4** NESTS - PREPARATION TIME: **10 MINUTES** - COOKING TIME: **1 HOUR**

INGREDIENTS FOR THE PAVLOVA • 90 ml aquafaba • 5 ml vanilla extract • 5 ml lemon juice • 2 g (½ tsp) guar gum • 80 g granulated sugar • Yuzu zest (optional) • 80 g icing sugar • Vegan chantilly cream • Amarena cherries in syrup

Method: Preheat the oven to 120°C/250°F/gas ½. Pour the aquafaba, vanilla extract and lemon juice into the stand mixer. Whisk at full power and sprinkle in the guar gum. Leave to whisk for a few minutes. When the mix becomes frothy and white, but hasn't yet formed soft peaks, gradually add the granulated sugar. Whisk for 3 to 5 minutes until it forms soft peaks. Add the yuzu zest and finish by gradually adding the icing sugar. Leave to whisk for 15 seconds longer and, then, use to fill a pastry bag with a thick nozzle (star or round). Pipe the pavlovas 3 cm high on a baking tray covered with baking paper. To get 4 equally sized pavlovas, draw circles around a bowl (11 cm in diameter) using a pencil. Then, make a dip in the middle, using the back of a spoon to form peaks around the edges, like a well. Cook for 1 hour, without opening the oven. Once the meringues are cooked, leave to cool and rest for a few hours. Fill the pavlovas with vegan chantilly cream and add some amarena cherries with a drizzle of syrup on top. Add a dusting of icing sugar and serve.

Comments: Yuzu is a Japanese citrus fruit with a similar taste to mandarin and bergamot. You can find it in Japanese shops during the autumn.

PARISIAN
WAFFLES

When you think about it, you can eat waffles at any time of day. For breakfast, brunch, as a dessert, tea time or for a midnight feast. Plain with just a dusting of sugar, or topped with chantilly cream, chocolate spread, chestnut cream or other delights, they're always great.

FOR **15** WAFFLES - PREPARATION TIME: **10 MINUTES**
COOKING TIME: **4 MINUTES**

INGREDIENTS • 170 ml soya milk • 5 ml vanilla extract • 120 ml vegetable oil • 160 g strong bread flour • 1 pinch unrefined fine salt • 80 ml aquafaba • 1 dash lemon juice • 30 g icing sugar • 1 g (⅓ tsp) cream of tartar

Method: Mix the soya milk, vanilla extract and oil in a bowl. Place the flour and salt in a separate bowl and pour the milk/vanilla/oil mixture over, whisking until you have a smooth mixture. Set aside.

Add the lemon juice to the aquafaba and mix in the stand mixer. Once the mixture becomes foamy, add the icing sugar and cream of tartar. Whisk at full power until stiff peaks form. Add to the previous mixture and gently fold using a spatula, always stirring in the same direction to incorporate.
The mixture is now ready to use. Pour a ladleful onto the waffle iron to cook. The cooking time will depend on your waffle iron, but on average 2 minutes are needed on each side.

Comments: The mixture should be used immediately. Unfortunately, it is not possible to prepare the mixture in advance, because the peaks will fall.

WHAT ABOUT THE
CHICKPEAS?

ROYAL
HUMMUS

Do not mess with this emblematic speciality! Hummus is THE thing that everyone loves, that gives you a huge appetite even if you're not hungry. It's incredibly addictive. And as everyone knows: 'Hummus one day, hummus every day!'

SERVES **4** - PREPARATION TIME: **15 MINUTES**

INGREDIENTS • 500 g cooked chickpeas • 100 ml cold water • 20 ml lemon juice • 3 g (½ tsp) unrefined fine salt • 3 g (1 tsp) ground cumin • 15 ml olive oil • 150 g tahini • 2 garlic cloves • Za'atar

Method: Set aside 10 chickpeas to use as decoration.
Pour the cold water, lemon juice, fine salt, cumin and olive oil into the bowl of a blender. Add the chickpeas, tahini and pressed garlic cloves.
Mix at full power for 5 minutes. The mixture should be completely smooth.
If it still looks a bit lumpy, add a splash of cold water and mix again.
Transfer the hummus onto a soup plate, add a generous dash of olive oil and sprinkle with za'atar. Garnish with the chickpeas and serve.

Comments: We use a pre-prepared Lebanese 'za'atar' mixture containing a mixture of herbs (wild thyme, marjoram, hyssop, sumac, sesame, salt). There are as many types of za'atar as regions in the Middle East. Therefore, there is no 'true' za'atar, just many different types depending on the region.

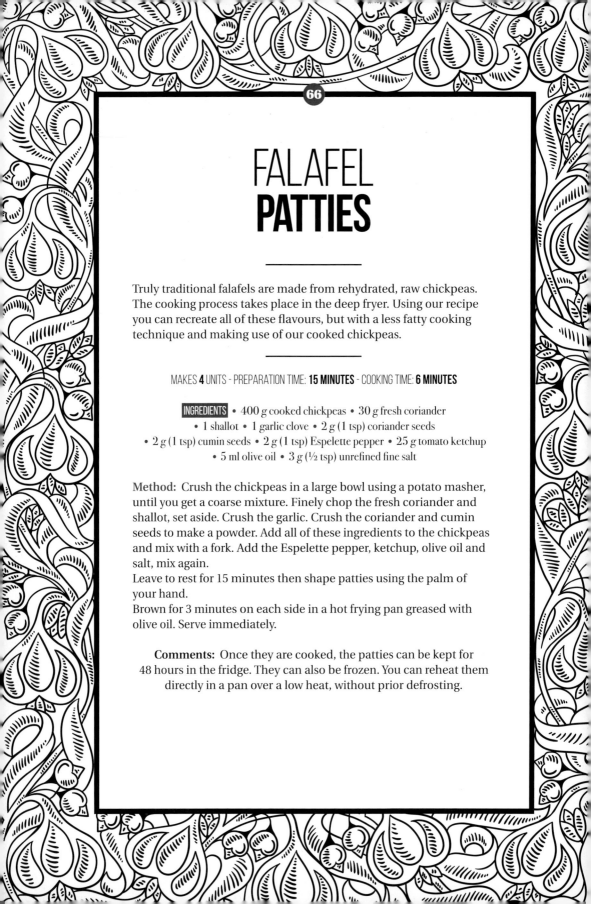

FALAFEL
PATTIES

Truly traditional falafels are made from rehydrated, raw chickpeas. The cooking process takes place in the deep fryer. Using our recipe you can recreate all of these flavours, but with a less fatty cooking technique and making use of our cooked chickpeas.

MAKES **4** UNITS - PREPARATION TIME: **15 MINUTES** - COOKING TIME: **6 MINUTES**

INGREDIENTS • 400 g cooked chickpeas • 30 g fresh coriander
• 1 shallot • 1 garlic clove • 2 g (1 tsp) coriander seeds
• 2 g (1 tsp) cumin seeds • 2 g (1 tsp) Espelette pepper • 25 g tomato ketchup
• 5 ml olive oil • 3 g (½ tsp) unrefined fine salt

Method: Crush the chickpeas in a large bowl using a potato masher, until you get a coarse mixture. Finely chop the fresh coriander and shallot, set aside. Crush the garlic. Crush the coriander and cumin seeds to make a powder. Add all of these ingredients to the chickpeas and mix with a fork. Add the Espelette pepper, ketchup, olive oil and salt, mix again.
Leave to rest for 15 minutes then shape patties using the palm of your hand.
Brown for 3 minutes on each side in a hot frying pan greased with olive oil. Serve immediately.

Comments: Once they are cooked, the patties can be kept for 48 hours in the fridge. They can also be frozen. You can reheat them directly in a pan over a low heat, without prior defrosting.

TANDOORI ROASTED
CHICKPEAS

———

Bored of the same old crisps and peanuts with your apéritif? Why not try roasted chickpeas for a change? It's original and nutritious.
Keep the great tastes, but without the saturated fats. Crunchy on the outside, melting in the middle, these tandoori roasted chickpeas are your new best friend.

———

SERVES **4** - PREPARATION TIME: **5 MINUTES** - COOKING TIME: **40 MINUTES**

INGREDIENTS • 500 g cooked chickpeas • 20 ml vegetable oil
• 15 ml coconut cream • 2 g (⅓ tsp) unrefined fine salt
• 5 g (2 tsp) tandoori spice mix

Method: Leave the chickpeas to dry in the open air overnight.
Preheat the oven to 190°C/375°F/gas 5.
Combine the oil, coconut cream, salt and half the tandoori spice mix in a mixing bowl. Add the chickpeas and mix everything thoroughly. Finish with the rest of the tandoori mix and combine one last time.
Spread on a baking tray covered with baking paper, making sure not to layer up the chickpeas. Bake for 40 minutes.
Leave to cool before serving.

Comments: Keep in a paper bag, in a dry place and
eat within 48 hours.

MEXICAN **SALAD**

Chickpeas are also delicious when eaten cold. Here is a Mexico-inspired recipe in which chickpeas replace black beans. The amounts provided here are for four starters, but it could also be served as a main for two people.

SERVES **4** - PREPARATION TIME: **15 MINUTES**

INGREDIENTS • 200 g cooked chickpeas • A few lettuce leaves • 35 ml olive oil • 2 g (1 tsp) smoked paprika • Pinch of salt • 1 g (½ tsp) chipotle chilli flakes • 15 ml cider vinegar • 5 ml jalapeño pepper sauce • ½ red onion • 1 lime • 250 g sweetcorn • 1 green pepper • 2 tomatoes • 1 avocado • ⅓ cucumber • Some tortilla chips

Method: Pour 5 ml olive oil into a hot frying pan, add the smoked paprika, a pinch of salt and the chipotle flakes. When the oil starts to brown, add the chickpeas, mix well and cook over a medium heat for 10 minutes, stirring regularly. Set aside. Pour 30 ml olive oil, the cider vinegar, jalapeño sauce and a pinch of salt into a small bowl. Mix vigorously using a fork. Set aside.
Finely chop the red onion and marinate in a bowl with the juice of the lime. Drain and rinse the sweetcorn. Wash and deseed the green pepper and chop into small pieces. Slice the tomatoes and dice the avocado. Cut the cucumber in half lengthways, remove the seeds and slice into thin slices.
Put a few washed lettuce leaves at the bottom of a salad bowl.
Add the rest of the ingredients and a few tortilla chips at random and pour the sauce over the top. Serve immediately.

Comments: If necessary, you can make this recipe in advance. You just have to add the tortilla chips and the sauce 5 minutes before serving.

CHICKPEA
CURRY

Indian cuisine is full of great ideas about how to cook legumes. It has to be said, plain chickpeas don't make the most glamorous of dishes and many people are reluctant to eat it in its most rudimentary form. However, in a curry, chickpeas are a real delight, mixing intense flavours and melt-in-your mouth textures.

SERVES **4** - PREPARATION TIME: **15 MINUTES** - COOKING TIME: **20 MINUTES**

INGREDIENTS • 1 red onion • 10 g fresh ginger • 1 garlic clove • 2 g (1½ tsp) coriander seeds • 2 g (1 tsp) cumin seeds • 20 ml rapeseed oil • 10 curry leaves • 9 g (1 tbsp) Madras curry powder • 400 ml coconut milk • 50 g (4 tbsp) tomato purée • 500 g cooked chickpeas • ½ lime • Pinch of fine salt • Fresh coriander

Method: Finely slice the onion, ginger and garlic. Using a pestle and mortar, crush the coriander and cumin seeds. In a large cooking pot, heat the rapeseed oil, add the crushed spices and curry leaves, and heat for 30 seconds before adding the chopped onion/ginger/garlic. Brown for 2 minutes then add the Madras curry powder, mix and add 50 ml of water. Reduce the heat for a few minutes before pouring in the coconut milk and adding the tomato purée. Season with salt, mix well. When the liquid starts to simmer, add the chickpeas, cover and cook over a low heat for 20 minutes. Add the juice of half a lime, mix and serve. Scatter fresh coriander leaves over as a garnish. Basmati rice makes a perfect accompaniment to this dish.

Comments: Madras curry is a fairly hot spice mix with deliciously spicy notes. If you are sensitive to these types of spices, we recommend a mild curry spice so that you can still enjoy the dish.

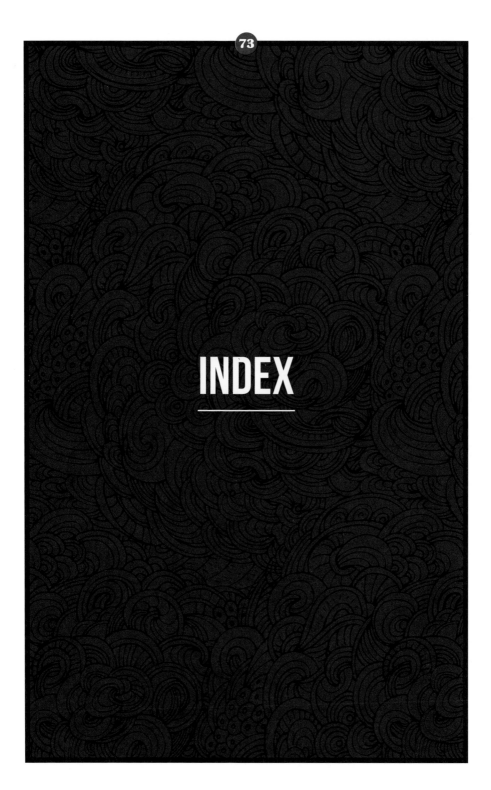

INDEX

USEFUL US CUPS/METRIC
CONVERSIONS

———

1 tablespoon (tbsp) = 3 teaspoons (tsp)
¹⁄₁₆ cup = 1 tablespoon
⅛ cup = 2 tablespoons
⅙ cup = 2 tablespoons + 2 teaspoons
¼ cup = 4 tablespoons
⅓ cup = 5 tablespoons + 1 teaspoon
⅜ cup = 6 tablespoons
½ cup = 8 tablespoons
⅔ cup = 10 tablespoons + 2 teaspoons
¾ cup = 12 tablespoons
1 cup = 48 teaspoons
1 cup = 16 tablespoons

———

1 tsp = 5 ml
1 tbsp = 15 ml
⅛ cup = 30 ml
¼ cup = 60 ml
½ cup = 120 ml
1 cup = 240 ml

———

1 tsp = 5 g
1 tbsp = 15 g
1oz = 25 g
1 cup cornflour = 120 g
1 cup flour = 120 g
1 cup flour, sieved = 110 g
1 cup granulated sugar = 200 g
1 cup icing sugar = 100 g
1 cup brown sugar = 180 g
1 cup semolina = 170 g

OTHER VEGAN COOKBOOKS PUBLISHED BY
GRUB STREET

Vegan Bible
Marie Laforêt
978-1-910690-07-9

Vegan BBQ
Nadine Horn & Jörg Mayer
978-1-910690-52-9

Raw Cakes
Caroline Fibaek
978-1-909808-05-8

**Vegan Recipes from
the Middle East**
Parvin Razavi
978-1-910690-37-6

**Homemade Vegan
Cheese, Yoghurt and Milk**
Yvonne Hölzl-Sing
978-1-911621-00-3

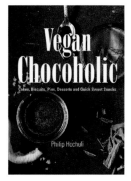

Vegan Chocoholic
*Cakes, Biscuits, Pies, Desserts
and Quick Sweet Snacks*
Philip Hochuli
978-1-910690-32-1

NOTES